# HIP-HOP & R&B

## Culture, Music & Storytelling

# Rihanna

# HIP-HOP & R&B

## Culture, Music & Storytelling

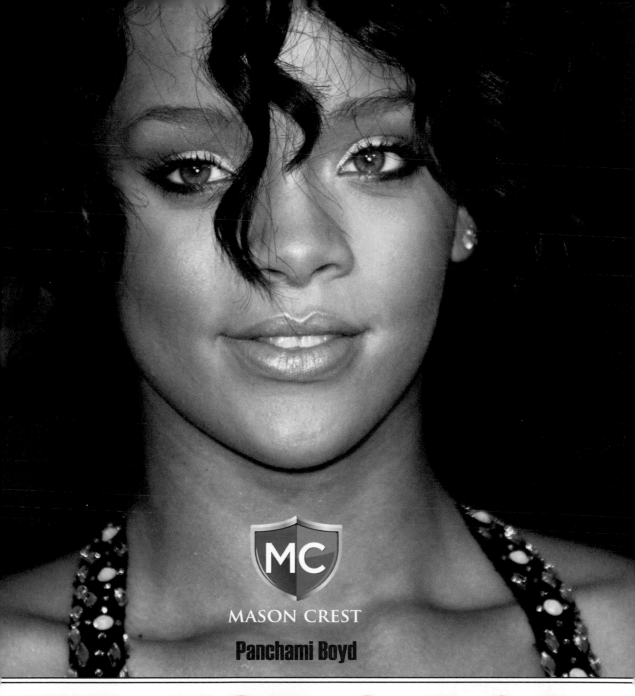

MASON CREST

Panchami Boyd

# HIP-HOP & R&B
*Rihanna*

& Storytelling

Mason Crest
450 Parkway Drive, Suite D
Broomall, Pennsylvania 19008
(866) MCP-BOOK (toll free)

First printing
9 8 7 6 5 4 3 2 1

hardback: 978-1-4222-4185-1
series: 978-1-4222-4176-9
ebook: 978-1-4222-7627-3

Library of Congress Cataloging-in-Publication Data

Names: Boyd, Panchami, author.
Title: Rihanna / Panchami Boyd.
Description: Broomall, PA : Mason Crest, 2018. | Series: Hip-hop & R&B:
culture, music & storytelling.
Identifiers: LCCN 2018020775 (print) | LCCN 2018021054 (ebook) | ISBN
    9781422276273 (eBook) | ISBN 9781422241851 (hardback) | ISBN
    9781422241769 (series)
Subjects: LCSH: Rihanna, 1988---Juvenile literature. |
Singers--Biography--Juvenile literature.
Classification: LCC ML3930.R44 (ebook) | LCC ML3930.R44 B69 2018 (print) |
    DDC 782.42164092 [B] --dc23
LC record available at https://lccn.loc.gov/2018020775

Developed and Produced by National Highlights, Inc.
Editor: Susan Uttendorfsky
Interior and cover design: Annalisa Gumbrecht, Studio Gumbrecht
Production: Michelle Luke

## QR CODES AND LINKS TO THIRD-PARTY CONTENT

# CONTENTS

## KEY ICONS TO LOOK FOR:

**Words to understand:** These words with their easy-to-understand definitions will increase the reader's understanding of the text while building vocabulary skills.

**Sidebars:** This boxed material within the main text allows readers to build knowledge, gain insights, explore possibilities, and broaden their perspectives by weaving together additional information to provide realistic and holistic perspectives.

**Educational videos:** Readers can view videos by scanning our QR codes, providing them with additional educational content to supplement the text. Examples include news coverage, moments in history, speeches, iconic sports moments, and much more!

**Text-dependent questions:** These questions send the reader back to the text for more careful attention to the evidence presented there.

**Research projects:** Readers are pointed toward areas of further inquiry connected to each chapter. Suggestions are provided for projects that encourage deeper research and analysis.

**Series of glossary of key terms:** This back-of-the-book glossary contains terminology used throughout this series. Words found here increase the reader's ability to read and comprehend higher-level books and articles in this field.

# Chapter 1

# Highlights Reel—Rihanna's Greatest Moments

Rihanna has produced eight studio albums, over a hundred of her singles have reached the *Billboard* Top 100 Chart, and more than ten of those singles have secured the number one spot. Overall, more than 54 million albums and approximately 210 million singles worldwide have been sold. Her tremendously successful career has affected several facets of the music industry in a profound way.

Even at a young age, Rihanna became a global icon, an international musical sensation, a successful businesswoman, and a promising actress. Highlighted throughout this chapter are noteworthy moments, singles, and albums that have shaped her hip-hop career into what it is today.

## Rihanna's Playlist

### MUSIC OF THE SUN
*(Released August 12, 2005)*

Rihanna's initial album sold over 600,000 copies in the United States and successfully launched her career as a music artist. Of particular importance is the first lead single,

Scan the code to watch *Pon de Replay*, the critically acclaimed lead single from Rihanna's first album

Scan the code to watch *S.O.S.*, one of the lead singles from Rihanna's second album, A Girl Like Me

called *Pon de Replay*. This dancehall song remains a fan favorite to this day.

## Collaborations

- *Here I Go Again*, featuring J-Status
- *You Don't Love Me (No, No, No)*, featuring Vybz Kartel
- *Rush*, featuring Kardinal Offishall
- *There's a Thug in Me*, featuring-J Status
- *Pon de Replay (Remix)*, featuring Elephant Man

# A Girl Like Me

## *(Released April 11, 2006)*

Rihanna's second album included two number one singles, *S.O.S.* and *Unfaithful*, both of which further expanded her fan base. The album sold over 1.4 million copies in the United States and received overwhelmingly positive reviews. It was certified Platinum by the Recording Industry Association of America (RIAA) in July 2006, just a few months after the album was released. The album peaked at the number five spot on *Billboard's* Top 200 Chart.

## Collaborations

- *Dem Haters,* featuring Dwane Husbands
- *Break It Off,* featuring Sean Paul

- *Crazy Little Thing Called Love,* featuring J-Status

- *If It's Loving That You Want—Part 2,* featuring Cory Gunz

## GOOD GIRL GONE BAD
### *(Released June 5, 2007)*

Though Rihanna's first two albums were generally well-received, GOOD GIRL GONE BAD is the one that many critics claim launched her to international success and fame, selling over 2.5 million copies in the United States and leading to her first Grammy win. It included hits and well-known singles like *Don't Stop The Music*. One single, *Umbrella*, remained at the top spot on the United Kingdom chart for eleven consecutive weeks.

The album was also remixed and reissued under the name GOOD GIRL GONE BAD: REDLOADED. This new release featured three new singles. Two of the singles from this version of the album were *Disturbia* and *Take a Bow*, and both reached number one status on the *Billboard* Top 100 Chart.

## Collaborations

- *Umbrella,* featuring Jay-Z

- *Hate That I Love You,* featuring Ne-Yo

Scan the code to watch the music video for *Umbrella* featuring Jay-Z

Scan to watch the music video for *Russian Roulette*, one of the lead singles off the album RATED R

# RATED R
*(Released November 23, 2009)*

The album RATED R marked a turn toward a more mature tone, as compared to her past work. It sold over 1 million copies in the United States, selling over 180,000 copies in its first week. *Rude Boy*, a lead single off the album, reached number one status and remained there for five consecutive weeks.

The album itself was deeply personal and original, with themes to empower women and girls. The album has sold over 1.5 million copies in the United States. It was a critical success at the time of its release, evidenced by the fact it reached number one status in eight countries worldwide.

## Collaborations

- *Hard,* featuring Young Jeezy
- *Rockstar 101,* featuring Slash
- *Photographs,* featuring will.i.am

# LOUD
*(Released November 16, 2010)*

Rihanna's fifth album sold over 1.8 million copies in the United States and over 8 million copies worldwide. Within its first week, more than 200,000 copies were purchased and it was released to number three on the *Billboard*

Top 200 Chart. A lead single, *Only Girl (In the World)*, won the Grammy Award for Best Dance Recording, while another, *S&M*, became Rihanna's tenth number one single—resulting in her being the youngest artist at the time to have ten number one singles.

Overall, the album was a critical success. It featured several up-tempo music genres, including dancehall, R&B, and electro-pop.

## Collaborations

- *What's My Name*, featuring Drake

- *Raining Men*, featuring Nicki Minaj

- *Love the Way You Lie (Part II)*, featuring Eminem

## TALK THAT TALK
*(Released November 21, 2011)*

Rihanna employed an interesting method to promote this album by encouraging fans to complete games to unlock new information. Winning games also gave fans access to new singles. TALK THAT TALK sold over 1 million copies in the United States and more than 5 million worldwide, reaching number one spots in five different countries around the world. The album's success highlighted her gamified promotion approach as a success at attracting new audiences worldwide.

Scan here to watch the music video for *Only Girl (In the World)*

Scan here to listen to *Talk That Talk*, the title song of Rihanna's sixth studio album

Scan to watch *Diamonds*, which has over 1 billion views on YouTube

## Collaborations

- *We Found Love*, featuring Calvin Harris
- *Talk That Talk*, featuring Jay-Z

## UNAPOLOGETIC
*(Released November 19, 2012)*

Selling over 1.2 million copies throughout the United States made UNAPOLOGETIC her first number one album. It sold 238,000 copies in its first week and eventually went on to win a Grammy for Best Urban/Contemporary Album. The album has sold over 4 million copies worldwide and is considered a critical success.

## Collaborations

- *Numb*, featuring Eminem
- *Loveeeeeee Song*, featuring Future
- *Right Now*, featuring David Guetta
- *Stay*, featuring Mikky Ekko
- *Nobody's Business*, featuring Chris Brown

## ANTI
*(Released January 28, 2016)*

After selling 166,000 copies during the first week of sales, ANTI became Rihanna's second consecutive album to reach number one status on the *Billboard* Top 100 Chart. Its lead single,

*Work*, featuring Canadian rapper Drake, reached number one status on *Billboard's* Hot 100 singles chart ranking within thirty-six hours of its release on iTunes.

The lead single's success also made Rihanna one of the top five artists with at least ten top singles in *Billboard's* Hot 100 history. Together with Samsung, 1 million copies of the album were available for free to download—a definite perk for excited fans of Rihanna's.

## Collaborations

- *Consideration*, featuring SZA

- *Work*, featuring Drake

*Drake at the 52nd Annual Grammy Awards, Press Room, Staples Center, Los Angeles, CA*

# Tours Bring Music to the People

Rihanna has not shied away from the spotlight since she participated in a high school talent show and won. She has headlined six world tours, co-headlined a tour with Eminem, and performed live at award shows, fashion shows, and a number of other events.

## RIHANNA: LIVE IN CONCERT *Tour*

Rihanna's first headline tour promoted both MUSIC OF THE SUN and A GIRL LIKE ME. Between July through September of 2006, she performed at over thirty shows throughout North America. She worked hard on the choreography and played her best-selling singles, like *S.O.S.* and *We Ride*.

## GOOD GIRL GONE BAD *Tour*

This worldwide circuit in support of GOOD GIRL GONE BAD included shows for her loyal fans across North America, Europe, Asia, Oceania, and Africa, making it Rihanna's first world tour. Over eighty performances were completed from September 2007 to January 2009.

A number of musicians joined Rihanna on the tour, including Akon as the opening act in

Scan to watch Rihanna performing live in Central Park, New York, at the Global Citizen Festival in 2016

select North American shows, and Ciara for shows in the United Kingdom.

This tour was considered to be an upbeat party, as fans and critics alike enjoyed dancing along to Rihanna's greatest hits.

## Last Girl on Earth *Tour*

Rihanna's third tour, in support of her album Rated R, grossed $40 million. While preparing, Rihanna explained her plans to make the shows edgy, new, and exciting:

*We've been prepping for the tour for a few months now, coming out with different ideas and cool things that we can do, things that we've never seen before, daring things—but now is when we really start with the rehearsal and we get into the nitty-gritty and the details of everything. I love taking risks. I'm not afraid of the unknown.*

The tour lasted from April 2010 to March 2011 and included a total of sixty-five shows across North America, Australia, and Europe.

Scan here to watch
a trailer for the
concert DVD
from the LOUD Tour

## LOUD *Tour*

From June to December 2011, Rihanna promoted her fifth studio album, LOUD, on this worldwide tour. With ninety-eight shows throughout North America, South America, and Europe, the tour grossed $90 million. Along with being considered a critical success, the journey finished off with the release of a live tour DVD. It was recorded from a show at the O2 in London and the DVD's title was *Loud Tour Live at the O2*. Special guests Drake, Kanye West, and Jay-Z were featured in various shows, adding to the excitement of the overall tour.

# 777 *World Tour*

Ahead of the release of her album UNAPOLOGETIC, Rihanna headlined a tour in November 2012: seven concerts in seven countries in the seven days leading up to her seventh studio album. This incredibly innovative promotion paid off, as UNAPOLOGETIC became her first number one album.

A year after the tour, Rihanna released a documentary about the concert experience. The film aired on Fox Network in May 2013, and was released on DVD later in the same month. Along with songs from various shows from the tour, the film gave fans tidbits of Rihanna preparing for the tour, behind-the-scenes moments, and flashes of Rihanna interacting with fans.

## DIAMONDS *World Tour*

The Diamonds World Tour, after the release of Rihanna's album UNAPOLOGETIC, broke several records. The circuit started in March and ended in November 2013, with ninety-six shows across North America, Africa, the Middle East, Asia, Oceania, and Europe. It grossed over $130 million and featured guest artists like David Guetta, A$AP Rocky, and others.

One of the records broken was that Rihanna was the youngest female artist to sell out a show at National Stadium in France, and Millennium

Scan here to watch a promotion video for her 777 World Tour

As part of the tour and album promotions, Rihanna created a series of eight videos entitled *ANTI diaRy*. Scan here to watch one

and Twickenham Stadiums in the UK. This incredible, groundbreaking success further demonstrated Rihanna's incredible star power.

## Anti *World Tour*

To promote this studio album, the tour performed seventy-five shows across North America, Asia, and Europe, grossing over $100 million and featuring guest artists like Travis Scott, The Weeknd, and Big Sean. Both the tour and Anti were highly anticipated, as Rihanna had taken a break between music projects to pursue other initiatives.

# Noteworthy Collaborations

### *If I Never See Your Face Again, featuring Maroon 5*
*(Released May 02, 2008)*

As one of Rihanna's first collaborations outside of her own albums, this song was an immediate hit. It was on the Reloaded version of her Good Girl Gone Bad album. Rihanna, a longtime fan of Maroon 5, was honored to receive the opportunity to work with the band. Similarly, Adam Levine, the lead singer of Maroon 5, felt that there was a genuine magic between the two artists and enjoyed the collaboration experience. The music video for this pop and R&B song has over 100 million views on YouTube.

Scan here to watch
the music video
for *If I Never See
Your Face Again*

## *Love The Way You Lie, featuring Eminem*

### (Released June 10, 2010)

There are over 1 billion views of this
single on YouTube, which was released
as part of Eminem's studio album Recovery.
It sold over 6 million copies in the
United States and remained on the
number one spot of *Billboard's* Top 100

Chart for seven consecutive weeks.

Actor Megan Fox and British actor Dominic Monaghan were both featured in the video. The director, Joseph Kahn, commented that Megan Fox's work in the video was particularly powerful and helped give the project greater impact.

### FourFiveSeconds, featuring Kanye West and Paul McCartney
*(Released January 25, 2015)*

This catchy song, which Rihanna co-wrote with Paul McCartney, topped the *Billboard* Top 100 Chart and reached number one status in over five countries worldwide. It wasn't included on an album; instead, Rihanna released it immediately for digital download. The creative but unlikely combination of singers—including backup by Wilson Phillips—surprised fans and critics, contributing to its success.

### This Is What You Came For, featuring Calvin Harris
*(Released April 29, 2016)*

Dynamic duo Calvin Harris and Rihanna came back to work together on this hit single. It became Rihanna's twelfth number one track and is certified Platinum in the United States. The song was co-

Scan here to watch the black-and-white music video for *FourFiveSeconds*

written by Calvin Harris and singer Taylor Swift.

Reviews of the song were generally mixed, and some critics believed it was not as impressive as their previous collaboration, *We Found Love*. Even so, Rihanna's vocals on the rack were thoroughly praised.

## Wild Thoughts, featuring DJ Khaled and Bryson Tiller
*(Released June 16, 2017)*

This lead single from DJ Khaled's album Grateful, Wild Thoughts is a wildly successful song, as it reached number one status on *Billboard's* Hot R&B/Hip-Hop Songs Chart. It peaked at number two in Canada and Australia, and on *Billboard's* Hot 100 in the United States. The song samples Carlos Santana's *Maria*, and Carlos was honored by the choice of his song. He stated that the artists involved brought a "new dimension" to the song, while still maintaining the "groove and essence" of Santana's original.

## *Loyalty, featuring Kendrick Lamar*
*(Released June 20, 2017)*

*Loyalty*, from Kendrick Lamar's sixth studio album, is considered a standout single from the album. When asked about Rihanna and his decision to collaborate with her, Kendrick Lamar had nothing but positives to say:

> *I love everything about her. Her artistry, how she represents women to not only be themselves but to express themselves the way she expresses herself through music and how she carries herself, I love everything about her so I always wanted to work with her.*
>
> **Kendrick Lamar**

Scan the code to listen to *Wild Thoughts*, a single that was lauded as the song of summer 2017 by some critics

The single reached number one on *Billboard's* Rhythmic Songs airplay chart, giving Lamar his second number one hit and Rihanna her nineteenth number one hit on this chart.

Scan here to watch the music video for *Loyalty*

*Kendrick Lamar (American hip-hop recording artist) performs at the 2014 Heineken Primavera Sound Festival*

**corporal:** a military term describing a noncommissioned officer ranking above a private first class in the United States Army, or lance corporal in the Marines, and below a sergeant or a similar rank in the armed services of other countries.

**debut:** a first public appearance on a stage, on television, etc., or the beginning of a profession or career; the first appearance of something, like a new product.

**demo:** a recording of a new song, or of one performed by an unknown singer or group, distributed to disc jockeys, recording companies, etc., to demonstrate the merits of the song or performer.

**discography:** a descriptive list of recordings by category, composer, performer, or date of release.

**single:** a music recording having two or more tracks that is shorter than an album, EP, or LP; also, a song that is particularly popular independent of other songs on the same album or by the same artist.

# Chapter 2

# The Road to the Top—Growing Up & Getting Educated to Gain Success

## Growing Up & Getting Educated

Rihanna was born in the Parish of Saint Michael on Barbados in 1988 under her birth name of Robyn Fenty. Her parents, Monica Braithwaite and Ronald Fenty, had a rocky relationship as Rihanna grew up, which affected her health as a child. The stress from the relationship gave her chronic headaches.

She has two younger brothers and three half-siblings. Following her parents' divorce, Monica went to work full time while Rihanna took care of her younger brother, starting when she was nine years old. She remembers feeling like she had to mature quickly and become a second mother to him.

Despite a rough childhood, Rihanna grew up strong, with a thick skin and a determined personality. When she eventually left Barbados to launch her music career, she says she knew it was exactly what she wanted to do—and was prepared to do everything it took to become successful and pursue her dreams. It's clear now that her hard work, passion, and dedication has paid off, as she is one of the most influential and best-selling artists in the music industry.

Rihanna attended Combermere High School, and at age fifteen, she performed in and won her school's talent show, singing Mariah Carey's hit *Hero*. In high school, Rihanna was a Barbados Cadet Corps trainee, eventually reaching the rank of **corporal**. Though she eventually dropped out of high school to pursue her music career, she often mentions the importance of education in her speeches, and expresses how she wishes she had gone to college.

**Shontelle & Rihanna's Shocking Connection**—When Rihanna was a cadet in high school, her drill sergeant was Shontelle, best known for her Platinum **single** *Impossible*. Shontelle joked that as a drill sergeant, she got to tell Rihanna to "drop and give her ten (push-ups)." Jokes aside, Shontelle was happy to know that she and Rihanna, both from a small town in Barbados, were able to find success in the music industry in their own ways.

## New Beginnings

Rihanna's career as a musician began when she performed for music producers Evan Rogers and Carl Sunken. In 2003, they were on vacation in Barbados and saw Rihanna sing in a chance concert and, later, at a private audition. At sixteen years old, her skills impressed these two New York City professionals, and she moved to America to continue working in the music industry with Rogers. This connection, and her performance, jumpstarted her music career.

Rapper and musician Jay-Z eventually heard the **demo** tape of her future hit **debut single**, *Pon de Replay*. At the time, Jay-Z was the president of Def Jam Records, and he invited Rihanna to audition for a spot with the label. Her performance impressed him so much that he signed her on to Def Jam Records almost immediately, and her **discography** began with his label.

*Jay-Z performing at a concert in Toronto*

**Fast Fact 2:**

**Even though Jay-Z was relatively quick to sign Rihanna onto his label, it wasn't without some concerns.** It is reported that when he first heard the demo, he believed that *Pon de Replay* was too big for a newcomer, and he was skeptical about giving it to her. However, immediately after Rihanna's audition, he was certain that she was right for the song—and right for Def Jam Records. Since then, their professional and personal friendship has remained strong.

# Becoming a Star

It might seem as though Rihanna became a star quickly. After all, being discovered by popular music producers and getting signed on to Jay-Z's label with are both incredible, once-in-a-lifetime feats. However, it was Rihanna's raw talent, hard work, and versatility that truly led to her success.

Her **debut single** *Pon de Replay* was released May 25, 2005. It reached number two on *Billboard's* Top 100 Chart and charted within the top five spots in more than five other countries around the world. It was a pop sensation that included dancehall elements, connecting Rihanna back to her roots. Moreover, the single was certified Platinum by the Recording Industry Association of America (RIAA), the premiere certifying body for the music industry in the United States.

Her critical success started with that sensational single, and it has grown since then. Only time will tell where her success continues to take her, and which other avenues she will explore as an artist.

**Text-Dependent Questions:**

❶ What song did Rihanna perform during her high school talent show?

❷ What record label first launched Rihanna's career?

❸ What was Rihanna's debut single, and when was it released?

 **Research Project:**

Rihanna's first **single** went Platinum, and she has received several accolades from RIAA since then. Take a look at the RIAA website (https://www.riaa.com/) and explore the various types of certifications an artist

can receive. Write down the requirements needed to achieve each of the certifications. Then, find out how often Rihanna has been certified by the RIAA to date. Explain why the RIAA is important to artists and fans. Finally, research and describe at least three other ways an artist's success is understood around the world.

**brand:** a particular product or a characteristic that serves to identify a particular product; a brand name is one having a well-known and usually highly regarded or marketable word or phrase.

**cameo:** also called a cameo role; a minor part played by a prominent performer in a single scene of a motion picture or a television show.

**diversity:** the inclusion of individuals representing more than one national origin, color, religion, socioeconomic level, sexual orientation, etc.

**endorsement:** money earned from a product recommendation, typically by a celebrity, athlete, or other public figure.

**entrepreneur:** a person who organizes and manages any enterprise, especially a business, usually with considerable initiative and at financial risk.

**voice actor:** an actor who provides off-screen voice-overs for dubbed films, commercials, or radio dramas; someone who creates the speech and/or sings as characters in animated films, video games, etc.

# Chapter 3

# More Than a Musician

With her feet firmly planted in the music industry, Rihanna has become one of the most best-selling artists of all time. Her successes in music and her **entrepreneurial** spirit have enabled her to complete projects in a number of other industries. Through ventures in fashion, cosmetics, film, and more, Rihanna's star power and international reach have grown exponentially.

## Fashion-Forward Thinker

Rihanna's personal clothing style has always been lauded for being provocative, innovative, and fashion-forward. It comes as no surprise that she has taken on fashion projects through several ventures. One of her most notable looks occurred at the Council of Fashion Designers of America (CFDA) Awards in 2014, when she wore a fishnet bodysuit covered in Swarovski crystals.

Scan here to watch Rihanna discuss her style, makeup needs, and more as part of a November 2013 *Glamour* cover story

She's also been one to watch at the Met Gala, a fundraising party for the Metropolitan Museum of Art's Costume Institute. Each year, Rihanna appears in elegant and innovative looks. A number of magazines and fashion experts have complimented her daring fashion choices.

Her eye for fashion in her personal life, and how she became a fashion icon through her style choices on the red carpet, makes her the perfect candidate for partnerships with fashion leaders.

## Fenty x Puma

One of her most notable fashion projects has been a partnership with shoe designer Puma, for the Fenty Puma collection. Through the partnership, and as Creative Director at Puma, Rihanna has designed a number of shoes in a variety of styles that are sold online and in Puma stores. From slides to boots to sneakers, Rihanna creates something for everyone. As Puma's Creative Director, she can explore her capabilities as a designer further, along with fulfilling her **entrepreneurial** spirit.

When Rihanna released her third version of the Puma Creeper in May 2016, *Vanity Fair* said the "Puma Suede creeper—a sneaker with a flat, thick-soled, 'creeper' platform attached … [is] expected to sell out as quickly as the first two releases." The first release "sold out online within three hours of its pre-sale launch." They also said Rihanna has great taste, with a very clear vision of what she wants to create.

The excitement expressed by people to purchase footwear designed by Rihanna isn't only because her name is attached to them. She's committed to making the footwear she designs stylish, functional, and trendy.

Rihanna's Fenty x Puma Fall 2017 collection, released September 28, 2017, is sold online, as well as through a special pop-up bus that stopped in two New York City locations. Fans enjoyed an exciting opportunity to enjoy Rihanna's latest from Fenty Puma in person.

This release also spotlights Rihanna's commitment to making her products accessible in innovative ways.

## Stance

Through a partnership with Stance, Rihanna has designed a number of sock collections. These "Rihanna Socks" feature some of her most iconic fashion looks from various red carpets and music videos, and other "punk-goth" styles. Proceeds from all sales go toward Rihanna's charity organization, the Clara Lionel Foundation, which was founded in 2012 and named after her grandparents, Clara and Lionel Braithwaite.

**Fast Fact 3:**

**Stance** is an underwear and sock company committed to creating art for these overlooked garments. By taking an innovative approach to socks, the company has managed to solidify its **brand** across forty countries. With its focus on comfort, design, creativity, and freedom, it is not surprising that Rihanna chose to partner with them.

# Makeup: Something for Everyone

Alongside fashion, Rihanna has also made her mark in the cosmetics industry by working with big companies and by creating her own line of foundation, eye shadow, and other impressive makeup items.

## MAC

Through a partnership with MAC, a popular cosmetics company, Rihanna successfully launched her **brand** as a strong contender in the industry. Their collaboration began in 2013 with the RiRi Hearts MAC line, with four collections—one for each season. Products sold through the partnership include lipstick for the MAC Viva Glam line, lip gloss, eye shadow, nails, false eyelashes, and more.

When asked about the experience, Rihanna expressed being thrilled with the opportunity and by how much she learned:

 *I really got to play. There's so much to choose from, and you can mix different textures with different colors and different greens in different eye shadows. I learned so much about the detail of makeup and what makes things look different. What makes it apply different is really important. Every little detail is important.* 

Scan here to watch Rihanna discuss her partnership with MAC for her MAC Viva Glam lipstick shades

## Fenty Beauty

In September 2017, Rihanna released her new makeup line focusing on **diversity**—Fenty Beauty. Within weeks, the darker shades of its foundation line started to sell out. The forty-shade range of her foundations surprised and delighted fans, because it showed her dedication to providing makeup for all kinds of people.

Typically, darker shades of foundation are hard to find, which means that dark-skinned people who wish to buy makeup find it difficult to locate a perfect match. Through Fenty Beauty's excellent range, that struggle is diminished.

Foundation isn't the only thing that Fenty Beauty offers. Rihanna has also included blotting powder, highlighters, primer, and lipsticks—with more to come.

In a statement about why she decided to create Fenty Beauty, Rihanna offered these heartfelt thoughts:

> **66** *Fenty Beauty was created for everyone: for women of all shades, personalities, attitudes, cultures, and races. I wanted everyone to feel included. That's the real reason I made this line.* **99**

Shortly after the initial launch, Rihanna announced an extension of her makeup line—including new eye shadow, lipstick shades, and more—with a release date of October 2017. There are also plans to include a skin care line. It's evident that Rihanna is full of ideas on how to embrace the makeup industry and connect with fans on new levels: as a businesswoman and **entrepreneur**.

Watch Fenty Beauty's first official campaign video, featuring models like Duckie Thot, Halima Aden, Slick Woods, Indyamarie Jean, and other models of color

# Business Deals

Rihanna's star power has directly transferred into her ability to promote products through **endorsements**, resulting in higher sales. Research shows publishers of magazines that they will sell more copies when Rihanna is featured on the cover. Products also sell better when her name is attached.

The NPD Group, a company that researches the market power of celebrities, states that fans are 50 percent more likely to buy a certain **brand** of a product when it has been endorsed by their favorite celebrity. NPD measured this star power and assigned scores to various well-known entertainment personalities. Rihanna's score, the highest NPD has calculated, means that she has "3.7 times as many strong **brand endorsement** opportunities as the average big-name celebrity."

## Samsung

One of her most notable partnerships, aside from Puma and MAC, is with Samsung. In 2015, Rihanna signed a $25 million deal with the electronics company. They also subsequently paid for her ANTI World Tour. One million copies of her album ANTI were available to fans to download for free. Reportedly, Samsung paid for these as well. In tweets about the album's success, Rihanna thanked Samsung directly.

By connecting their **brand** to Rihanna, Samsung has successfully built a mutually beneficial partnership with Rihanna and her fans. This positive reception will only help both grow and flourish.

## Dior

Another noteworthy **endorsement** deal was signed between Rihanna and Dior. She designed sunglasses for the fashion powerhouse, and she has a strong connection with their ambassadors and designers. It is not uncommon to see Rihanna wearing Dior fashion on the red carpet, or to see her attending a Dior, fashion show.

Dior and Rihanna have also partnered on a charitable level. A portion of the sales of a 2017 fashion t-shirt from Dior, featuring the phrase "We Should All Be Feminists," will be donated to Rihanna's charity, the Clara Lionel Foundation. When asked to comment on the partnership, Grazia Chiuri, Artistic Director for Dior, stated

> 66 *Seeing artists such as Rihanna wearing the We Should All Be Feminists t-shirt showed me how important it is for women to advance their fight. My position in a house as influential as Dior, but also my role as a mother, reminds me every day of my responsibilities and the importance of my actions.* 99

Fast Fact 4:

**Fragrances by Rihanna**—Rihanna has created over ten fragrances offered for sale in different styles—ranging from roll-on, perfumes, scents for men, and gift boxes. They're available online, or in popular retailers like Kohl's and Macy's.

# Filmography: Delving into New Worlds as an Actor

Beyond her work as a musician, businesswoman, and entrepreneur, Rihanna has also successfully launched an acting career. With exciting upcoming projects and well-known roles already completed, Rihanna has created a solid standing for herself in the film industry.

## Battleship

Rihanna's debut film role was as Petty Officer Cora Raikes, a weapons specialist in the movie *Battleship*. The film, released on April 11, 2012, made $9.5 million on its opening day and $25.4 million during its opening weekend, resulting in over $200 million total internationally. The director of the film, Peter Berg, knew he wanted to cast Rihanna after seeing her in an emotional interview with Oprah and her versatility and comedic timing as a host on *Saturday Night Live*.

*Rihanna at the Australian premier of her movie* Battleship

She made the most of her first motion picture experience, telling Berg to not go easy on her. She was prepared to do anything to be good. Her high school cadet experience came in handy for the role, and she recalls using elements of the cadet etiquette and discipline she previously learned.

*Battleship* allowed Rihanna to discover that she could delve into worlds other than singing. The film experience made her "want to see what else (she) could do." *Battleship* instilled the acting bug in Rihanna, which has grown tremendously since her first role.

## Annie

In short **cameo** part in the film *Annie*, Rihanna played an interesting role—her character was featured in a "movie-within-a-movie." Ashton Kutcher and Mila Kunis were also featured in this movie-within-a-movie.

During one scene in *Annie*, the characters went to watch a movie and saw a preview for another movie starring Rihanna. Considered to be a scene of comedic gold, the parody scene added to her experience as an actor.

## Home

Physical acting isn't the only type of role that Rihanna has performed. Her first role as a **voice actor** was as Gratuity Tucci, aka Tip, in the film *Home*. The film was released on March 27, 2015, and Rihanna worked alongside several successful actors, including Jim Parsons, Steve Martin, and Jennifer Lopez. Though she said was nervous about messing up, she recalled the experience with positive feelings.

Rihanna's role helped DreamWorks Animation make history, with it being the company's third female protagonist. The movie is centered around Tip, a young girl who survives an alien abduction.

As Rihanna's first voice acting role, she was excited by everything she had to learn. The role itself was especially important to her because of what it meant for young girls. She was proud of her role, and stated,

 *It was both important to me and DreamWorks for this project to be as realistic as possible. We wanted little girls to feel empowered. Little girls of any size, shape, color, race: it didn't matter. We wanted girls to just feel strong and brave, empowered, beautiful, and that they can do anything. They can take charge of their life or situation, no matter what. I think we were really, really careful, especially with the animation, to make sure that she wore the right things. That her body was not unrealistic, you know, and I think for kids, that's really special for young girls.*

These inspiring words from Rihanna aren't surprising because of how much work she has put into making sure her other initiatives are inclusive and inspirational to both children and adults everywhere.

Fast Fact 5:

## As a child, Rihanna was often bullied about her skin color and body shape, and it contributed to her growing up with a thick skin. While working on the film *Home*, some of those feelings of being an outsider came back. Her words here serve as an inspiration to young people struggling with the same feelings—it's important to remember to always be yourself, no matter what people say.

## Bates Motel

Rihanna's first television role was a Marion Crane on *Bates Motel*. The show, and the characters, gave a new twist to the popular horror film *Psycho*. The executive producer of the show, Carlton Cuse, said that Rihanna had a tremendous amount of charisma and that she was a great addition to their team for the role. "She was so committed, she really worked hard, and she brought this open, vulnerable, completely in-the-moment quality to the character."

Rihanna, herself a fan of *Bates Motel*, felt that joining the show's cast was a dream come true. Executive producers called the match between Rihanna and the program a "perfect collision of creativity and fate."

## Valerian and the City of a Thousand Planets

In the 2017 science fiction film *Valerian and the City of a Thousand Planets*, Rihanna played the role of Bubble. Most of her work was through motion-capture work, so while her movements were recorded via computer, her physical form on the movie was an intergalactic alien. A short portion of the film, however, did include screen time of Rihanna looking like herself.

Comments from critics about the film were generally harsh and negative. They called several of the plot points—and the actors within it—dull, bland, and predictable. Nonetheless, Rihanna received overwhelmingly positive reviews and was considered to be the most engaging part of the movie. Her performance in the role even resulted in her winning an acting award.

Rihanna's excitement in portraying Bubble in the movie became clear when she spoke about her experience. She enjoyed the opportunity to pursue something new and different. She beamed while saying,

 *I loved it. I thought it was really cool. Sci-fi movies are always really fun, and this one has such a modern twist. There's a lot of reality in this world that's not real, and that's why I think I was attached to it.*

It's worth mentioning that there is an unfortunate and notable lack of women of color in the science fiction film genre. Based on the highest grossing films as of 2014, only 14 percent of sci-fi and fantasy films had a female protagonist, and only 8 percent of films featured a person of color as a protagonist. This research also showed that not a single film included a female protagonist of color. Rihanna's portrayal of Bubble in the $180-million-budget film is historic, as it promotes a message of inclusion and opens up the opportunity for women of color to thrive in the science fiction genre.

## Ocean's 8

This upcoming exciting film project is due to be released in June 2018. Ocean's 8 is an all-female remake and spin-off of the 2001 movie Ocean's Eleven. The all-star cast for this highly anticipated film includes Rihanna, Sandra Bullock, Anne Hathaway, Mindy Kaling, Cate Blanchett, Sarah Paulson, Helena Bonham Carter, and Awkwafina.

Rihanna posted the cast's first image on her Twitter account in January 2017. The photo has over 100,000 likes, demonstrating that the anticipation for the movie is palpable.

The reason women are so excited about the film is that of the top 100 films in 2016, only 29 percent included protagonists who were women, despite the fact that during the same year, 54 percent of movie watchers were women. Motion pictures like Ocean's 8 allow women to see a version of themselves on screen—to feel included and represented. Perhaps even more upsetting is that only 14 percent of female protagonists were black, 6 percent were Asian, and 3 percent were Latina.

*Ocean's 8* offers a new perspective on old tropes, allowing a greater number of women to participate in and enjoy the action film genre. It's important for movies to show alternative perspectives to stay fresh and exciting, and *Ocean's 8* is one way that Hollywood is doing so.

## Upcoming Untitled Film Project with Lupita Nyong'o and Issa Rae

An untitled exciting new movie featuring Rihanna and Lupita Nyong'o was announced in May 2017, with an anticipated start date to begin shooting in 2018. The picture will be written by Issa Rae and directed by Ava DuVernay—making this upcoming film a surefire hit.

The concept all started with a post on Tumblr. A fan noted that an image of Rihanna and Lupita Nyong'o at the Miu Miu Fashion Show in 2014 "look[ed] like they're in a heist movie with Rihanna as the tough-as-nails leader/master thief and Lupita as the genius computer hacker." The post went viral and eventually made its way to both Rihanna and Lupita, and they said they were interested. Ava DuVernay and Issa Rae joined in, tweeting about their desire to participate as well.

After an aggressive bid for the rights to the movie, the project came to life. This fresh way of coming up with ideas for films— through social media—shows how much times have changed. Online posts can tumble into something bigger than themselves. Perhaps now fans will be more eager to share their ideas for new movies and TV shows online. After all, it may go viral and come to life!

## Cameos

Along with playing new characters, Rihanna has also played herself, singing her music in feature films. For example, her first **cameo** was in *Bring It On: All or Nothing*, in which she sang her hit *Pon de Replay*. Another fan-favorite cameo was a bit in *This Is The End*, where she played a version of herself in the apocalyptic movie. Her character in the star-studded film is memorable and hilarious.

## Rihanna: Triple Threat

Singer, dancer, and actor, Rihanna is a definite triple threat in the music and film industries. From this success, she has reaped several benefits, including awards and creative opportunities in fashion and makeup. Companies all over the world see how successful Rihanna is and want to partner with her to further their mutual accomplishments. Only time will tell how much further Rihanna will go in her journey within each of these industries. And which new industries she will work with!

# Text-Dependent Questions:

❶ In which film did Rihanna have a voice acting role?

❷ What film that Rihanna is going to be starring in started from an online post? Who else will be involved in the project?

❸ How many shades of foundation does Fenty Beauty currently offer?

# Research Project:

As this chapter notes, Rihanna generates extremely strong selling power, more so than many other celebrities. For this project, think of a new product or brand that she currently does not endorse. Explain how Rihanna and the brand you've selected could benefit from a partnership or **endorsement** deal. What would an advertisement campaign for your partnership idea look?

# Words to Understand

**humanitarian:**
a person who cares about people and who often participates in charity or does good work to show that care; a person who tries to make the world better through social reform.

**press conference:**
an interview or announcement given by a public figure to the press at an appointed time.

**vanguard:**
the forefront of an action or movement.

# Chapter 4

# Words and Lyrics—Building a Brand

## Award-Winning Artist

As any public figure knows, words matter. Speeches, presentations, interviews, and **press conferences** are preserved forever, especially in this online age. Rihanna is one such public figure who takes her responsibility as a role model and celebrity seriously. During her acceptance speeches for awards, she leaves fans and watchers feeling motivated and hopeful.

One noteworthy speech from Rihanna was the 2016 MTV Video Music Awards, on August 28, 2016, held in Madison Square Garden in New York and televised on MTV. Equally inspiring was her acceptance speech of Harvard University's "**Humanitarian** of the Year" Award on February 28, 2017.

## The Michael Jackson Video Vanguard Award

This coveted recognition, named after musician Michael Jackson, is a lifetime-achievement award honoring artists for their groundbreaking music videos. The accolade is presented at MTV's Video Music Awards show.

## MTV Video Music Awards

As you'll read, Rihanna has been commended for her work as a **humanitarian** and philanthropist. However, first and foremost, she is a musician, and the music industry absolutely rewards her hard work. One speech worth highlighting occurred at the VMAs in 2016, when she won the Michael Jackson **Vanguard** Award.

Drake, a friend and fellow musical artist, presented her with the award, candidly stating, "She's someone I've been in love with since I was 22 years old." He continued speaking very highly of Rihanna:

"She's one of my best friends in the world. All my adult life, I've looked up to her, even though she's younger than me."

In Rihanna's acceptance speech, she thanked her family and fans, and said all of her successes should be shared with her community. She beamed while she spoke.

Scan here to watch Drake's full speech presenting Rihanna with the Michael Jackson Vanguard Award

*My success started as my dream. But now my success is not my own. It's my family's. It's my fans. It's my country's. It's the Caribbean as a whole. It's women. It's black women.*

# Harvard Foundation for Interracial and Cultural Relations

Rihanna accepted Harvard University's **Humanitarian** of the Year Award in 2017. Her speech was both heartfelt and humorous, and reminded people of the importance of helping others. She founded the Clara Lionel Foundation in 2012, a charity committed to improving global health and education. Her commitment to this organization and helping others led to her winning this inspiring award.

Some of the most notable parts of her acceptance speech included her discussing her passion for helping others and her motivation to continue the same, which started from a young age. Her thoughtful, inspirational words are sure to motivate anyone to make a change in their community.

> *We're all human. And we all just want a chance: a chance at life, a chance in education, a chance at a future, really. And at Clara Lionel Foundation, our mission is to impact as many lives as possible, but it starts with just one. Just one.*
>
> *As I stare out into this beautiful room, I see optimism, I see hope, I see the future. I know that each and every one of you has the opportunity to help someone else. All you need to do is help one person, expecting nothing in return. To me, that is a* **humanitarian**.

Her final sentence is profound and particularly moving: "My grandmother always used to say if you've got a dollar, there's plenty to share."

Rihanna has made it a point to use her star power, brand image, and success to uplift others and inspire change in her community.

What she shared in her speech is a meaningful lesson that everyone can carry with them, regardless of gender or age.

Scan here to watch Rihanna's full, thought-provoking speech from Harvard University's Humanitarian of the Year Award

## Fast Fact 6:

**In honor of Rihanna,** several Harvard students spoke about her projects, her impact, and how she inspires them to make change. One student said, "Thank you, Rihanna, for inspiring us to use our abilities to 'work, work, work' and to exercise these abilities in the service of others."

It's clear that Rihanna affects people in profound ways, far beyond her chart-topping singles. How does she inspire you?

## Awards Won

Rihanna has been nominated for more than 500 awards and has won over 190 of them. These accolades and nominations come from her diverse activities, including music, fashion, film, and, as noted above, **humanitarian** efforts. Most commonly, she has won accolades in the hip-hop, pop, and R&B music genres.

# Here are several of her most exciting awards won.

## American Music Awards
Favorite Pop/Rock Female Artist | Won in 2008
Favorite Soul/R&B Album—Loud | Won in 2011
Favorite Soul/R&B Album—Talk That Talk | Won in 2012
Icon Award | Won in 2013
Favorite Soul/R&B Album—ANTI | Won in 2016
Favorite Soul/R&B Song—*Work*, featuring Drake | Won in 2016
Favorite Soul/R&B Female Artist | Won in 2007, 2008, 2010, 2013, 2015, and 2016

## BET Awards
Viewer's Choice Award—*Live Your Life*, featuring T.I. | Won in 2009
Viewer's Choice Award—*Hard*, featuring Young Jeezy | Won in 2010
Best Female R&B Artist | Won in 2011 and 2014
Best Collaboration—*Work*, featuring Drake | Won in 2016

## Billboard Music Awards
Female Artist of the Year | Won in 2006
Top Rap Song—*Love the Way You Lie*, featuring Eminem | Won in 2011
Top Female Artist | Won in 2011
Top R&B Song—*Diamonds* | Won in 2013
Top R&B Album—Unapologetic | Won in 2013
Top R&B Artist | Won in 2013
Billboard Chart Achievement Award | Won in 2016

## BRIT Awards
International Female Solo Artist | Won in 2011 and 2012

## CFDA Fashion Awards
Fashion Icon Award | Won in 2014

## FiFi Awards
Best Celebrity Fragrance—Nude by Rihanna | Won in 2014

## Footwear News Achievement Awards

Shoe of the Year—Fenty Puma Creeper | Won in 2016

## Glamour Magazine Awards

Woman of the Year | Won in 2009

## Grammy Awards

Best Rap/Sung Collaboration—*Umbrella*, featuring Jay-Z | Won in 2008

Best Rap Song and Best Rap/Sung Collaboration—*Run This Town*,
featuring Jay-Z and Kanye West | Won in 2010

\Best Rap/Sung Collaboration—*All of the Lights*, featuring
Kanye West, Kid Cudi, and Fergie | Won in 2012

Best Short Form Music Video—*We Found Love*, featuring Calvin Harris | Won in 2013

Best Urban Contemporary Album—UNAPOLOGETIC | Won in 2014

Best Rap/Sung Collaboration—*The Monster*, featuring Eminem | Won in 2015

Best Rap/Sung Collaboration – *Loyalty*, featuring Kendrick Lamar | Won in 2018

## Guinness Book of World Records

Most digital number one singles in the United States | Won in 2010

Female artist with the most U.S. number one singles in a year | Won in 2010

Most consecutive years of United Kingdom number one singles | Won in 2011

The Best-Selling Digital Artist | Won in 2012

Most consecutive weeks on United Kingdom singles chart
(multiple singles) | Won in 2013

## Harvard Foundation for Interracial and Cultural Relations

Humanitarian of the Year | Won in 2017

## iHeartRadio Music Awards

Hip-Hop/R&B Song of the Year—*Pour It Up* | Won in 2014

Song of the Year—*Stay*, featuring Mikky Ekko | Won in 2014

Artist of the Year | Won in 2014

Best Collaboration—*Work*, featuring Drake | Won in 2017

R&B Song of the Year—*Work*, featuring Drake | Won in 2017

Album of the Year—ANTI | Won in 2017

## MTV Movie Awards

Best Cameo—*This Is The End* | Won in 2014

## MTV Video Music Awards

Video of the Year—*Umbrella*, featuring Jay-Z | Won in 2007
Monster Single of the Year—*Umbrella*, featuring Jay-Z | Won in 2007
Best Pop Video—*We Found Love*, featuring Calvin Harris | Won in 2012
Michael Jackson Vanguard Award | Won in 2016

## MuchMusic Video Awards

International Video of the Year—*Don't Stop the Music* | Won in 2008

## People's Choice Awards

Favorite R&B Song—*Shut Up and Drive* | Won in 2008
Favorite Music Collaboration—*Run This Town*,
featuring Jay-Z and Kanye West | Won in 2010
Favorite Pop Artist | Won in 2011
Favorite Music Video, Favorite Song—*Love the Way You Lie*,
featuring Eminem | Won in 2011
Favorite R&B Artist | Won in 2012, 2013, and 2017

## Teen Choice Awards

Choice R&B Artist, Choice Breakout Artist Female | Won in 2006
Choice R&B Artist | Won in 2007
Choice Rap/Hip-Hop Track—*Love the Way You Lie,* featuring Eminem | Won in 2010
Choice Movie: Breakout Female—*Battleship* | Won in 2012

## YouTube Awards

50 Artists to Watch | Won in 2015

## Hard Work Pays Off

One incredible truth about Rihanna is that she works extremely hard for her success. From the day she decided to leave her home country to pursue a musical career to now, she has never shied away from challenges. She inspires her fellow artists and fans alike, and creates a space where everyone feels empowered to pursue their own dreams. Winning just one award is a remarkable achievement, and seeing the sheer number of awards she's won is exciting in itself. However, what is more inspiring is the way she commands the stage with her words in her acceptance speeches. She uses the

opportunities to connect with her audience, speak from the heart, and show genuine enthusiasm for what is to come.

People around the world are able to share in her joy when she wins an award, and they feel empowered to continue working passionately. By using her platform for something bigger than herself, Rihanna has been able to sustain and prolong her success, and it's likely that this will be the case for decades to come.

## Text-Dependent Questions:

❶ Who said the quote that Rihanna shared at the end of her acceptance speech for Harvard University's **Humanitarian** Award?

❷ What is the Michael Jackson **Vanguard** Award?

❸ Who presented Rihanna with the Michael Jackson Vanguard Award?

## Research Project:

In Rihanna's speech following winning the **Humanitarian** Award, she said, "Today I want to challenge each of you to make a commitment to help one person: one organization, one situation that touches your heart."

Select an issue that you care about (e.g., health, education). Find contact information for your local government representatives, both within your city and in your state, or the contact information for a non-profit organization that focuses efforts on the issue you've selected. Then draft a letter to an individual from your local government or your selected non-profit organization about why this issue matters to you and what you hope to see improve in your community. Explain the ways you hope they will plan to make a change. If you'd like, talk to a teacher, parent, or other responsible adult in your life to see if you can send your letter to the appropriate representative. Change starts with you!

## Words to Understand

**advocating:**
promoting, pleading for, or supporting a cause or proposal.

**ambassador:**
a diplomatic official serving as representative-in-residence by one government or sovereign to another, or to the United Nations; a person authorized to represent an organization.

**literacy:**
the quality or state of being literate, especially having the ability to read and write; having an education.

**mission statement:**
an official document that sets out the goals, purpose, and work of an organization.

**philanthropy:**
goodwill to fellow members of the human race; an active effort to promote human welfare.

# Building Up the Community to Make a Difference

## Spearheading Change

Rihanna believes that even though "the lack of access to education for children around the world is a massive problem ... that doesn't mean we should just throw up our hands in despair and surrender."

Through a number of projects, Rihanna has raised her voice for social good and firmly planted herself as a **philanthropist** who cares about everyone around her. Her efforts toward improving **literacy** and increasing access to education around the world are both commendable and inspiring.

## Clara Lionel Foundation

Because of Rihanna's strong feelings about education and other benefits for children, she created a charity organization to promote global change and goodness in 2012. The Clara Lionel Foundation, named for her grandparents Clara and Lionel Braithwaite, focuses on improving children's quality of life through health, education, arts, and culture. The organization echoes Rihanna's belief that all children deserve equal access to education. Its **mission statement** raises a voice for better health care around the world, and hopes to build

additional foundations to better lives around the world.

Scan the code to watch Rihanna discuss her reasons for starting the Clara Lionel Foundation, and her vision for its future

**Fast Fact 7:**

**Over 263 million children and youths are not in school around the world.** Sub-Saharan Africa has the highest rates of exclusion from education, with over a fifth of children between the ages of six and eleven not in school. Generally, older children—from fifteen to seventeen years old—are more likely to be out of school. Many of them are forced to pursue work instead. Girls are more likely to never set foot into a classroom—research shows that 5 million girls of primary school age will never get the chance to learn to read or write in primary school.

# Advocating for Education around the World

Both through her foundation and in other partnerships, Rihanna has become a global spokesperson for improved access to education worldwide.

## Global Partnership for Education and Global Citizen

Beginning in September 2016, the Clara Lionel Foundation partnered with both the Global Partnership for Education and Global Citizen. As the GPE Global **Ambassador**, Rihanna advocates for global education, and education for emergencies, among leaders and policymakers around the world. Her voice will be used to amplify the work of GPE and the Clara Lionel Foundation to focus on bringing better, more sustainable education to countries around the world.

## Meeting with the French President

Another effort by Rihanna to improve education came during a meeting with French President

Emmanuel Macron in July 2017. She spoke with him and the First Lady of France, Brigitte Macron, about the Clara Lionel Foundation and her commitment to providing education and health care to underserved communities around the world.

After the meeting, Rihanna tweeted, "Thank you Mr. President Emmanuel Macron and Madame First Lady for the incredible meeting and passion for global and girls education", indicating that a productive conversation took place.

## The Dollar Campaign

Through the Clara Lionel Foundation, Rihanna launched this drive in 2017 to fund education efforts in Malawi and help aspiring students attend school. The name came from her Humanitarian of the Year Award speech, where she mentioned her grandmother used to say, "If you've got a dollar, there's plenty to share."

The funds donated through The Dollar Campaign will assist in building schools in Malawi, buying books for students, and providing assistance to students for school supplies and tuition.

## Global Scholarship Program

Rihanna's foundation has also established a scholarship program for students from a number of countries, including Brazil, Barbados, Cuba, Haiti, and Jamaica. Through the Global Scholarship Program, older students can receive scholarships from the Clara Lionel Foundation after being accepted into accredited four-year colleges or universities in the United States.

Relieving the financial burden on these undergraduates allows them to focus on their schooling and make the most of their opportunities. Recipients receive anywhere between $5,000 to $50,000 to put toward their education.

# Improving Health Care for Better Quality of Life

In additional to education, improved access to better health care is a topic near to Rihanna's heart.

## Queen Elizabeth Hospital

To promote better care in Barbados, the Clara Lionel Foundation installed state-of-the-art machinery and paid for improved facilities at Queen Elizabeth Hospital. Rihanna's grandmother, Clara Braithwaite, had cancer, so this project was deeply personal for Rihanna. The new Clara Braithwaite Center for Oncology and Nuclear Medicine at the hospital aims to provide Barbados residents with high-quality cancer treatments through the improved technology.

## The Annual Diamond Ball

One creative way Rihanna raises funds for the Clara Lionel Foundation is through the Diamond Ball. This annual charity gala has been held in a number of different United States cities and always invites a number of celebrity guests and performers. Some of the celebrities who have attended or performed are Calvin Harris, Beyoncé, comedian Dave Chappelle, Kendrick Lamar, Leonardo DiCaprio, Jamie Foxx, and Lionel Richie.

All the money raised goes toward health-care initiatives, as well as education projects and micro-grants through the Clara Lionel Foundation. In 2014, the Diamond Ball raised $2 million, which increased to $3 million in 2015. At the third annual Diamond Ball gala in 2017, items including art pieces, white gold necklaces, and wine tastings were sold for anywhere between $80,000 and $100,000 each.

**Fast Fact 8:**

**Rihanna participates in a number of projects outside of her own foundation** that are dedicated to assisting others. She performed at the 2016 MusiCares Person of the Year Tribute to Lionel Richie. This social event raises money to provide services and resources to cover medical, financial, and personal emergencies. The services are available to individuals in the music industry who require emergency assistance.

## Using Her Power for Good

Rihanna has over 25 million subscribers on her YouTube channel, over 80 million likes on Facebook, over 70 million followers on Twitter, and over 50 million followers on Instagram. It's clear that she has an enormous number of fans, an incredibly great amount of star power, and a very strong public voice with which to get her messages out. She takes her social media platform very seriously, as is evident by her passionate voice in **advocating** for global health and education. The way Rihanna is quick to use both her social media presence and her platform to give a voice to those who many not be heard

is inspiring to all. It motivates her peers to assist in raising money for change, as seen in her Diamond Ball efforts, and among fans by acting as a positive role model to them.

Rihanna is an excellent role model because she shows us to follow our dreams and work hard, reminds us to be passionate about what we do, and demonstrates how we can be a force for change in our communities. We can each learn to be better people, citizens, and friends by watching the way she has changed the world—in more ways than one.

# Text-Dependent Questions:

❶ What is the Diamond Ball, and how much money did it raise in 2015?

❷ Which president did Rihanna meet with in 2017 to discuss education?

❸ What are the two main focus areas of the Clara Lionel Foundation—those it places the most importance on?

# Research Project:

Of the initiatives that the Clara Lionel Foundation focuses on, which one do you think is the most important? Why? How could you create a project—like Rihanna's Diamond Ball, or something similar—to raise awareness of this issue in your community and benefit those affected by it? What type of initiative could you run, perhaps with the help of people in your community?

# Series Glossary of Key Terms

**A&R:** an abbreviation that stands for Artists and Repertoire, which is a record company department responsible for the recruitment and development of talent; similar to a talent scout for sports.

**ambient:** a musical style that relies on electronic sounds, gentle music, and the lack of a regular beat to create a relaxed mood for the listener.

**brand:** a particular product or a characteristic that serves to identify a particular product; a brand name is one having a well-known and usually highly regarded or marketable word or phrase.

**cameo:** also called a cameo role; a minor part played by a prominent performer in a single scene of a motion picture or a television show.

**choreography:** the art of planning and arranging the movements, steps, and patterns of dancers.

**collaboration:** a product created by working with someone else; combining individual talents.

**debut:** a first public appearance on a stage, on television, or so on, or the beginning of a profession or career; the first appearance of something, like a new product.

**deejay (DJ):** a slang term for a person who spins vinyl records on a turntable; aka a disc jockey.

**demo:** a recording of a new song, or of one performed by an unknown singer or group, distributed to disc jockeys, recording companies, and the like, to demonstrate the merits of the song or performer.

**dubbed:** something that is named or given a new name or title; in movies, when the actors' voices have been replaced with those of different performers speaking another language; in music, transfer or copying of previously recorded audio material from one medium to another.

**endorsement:** money earned from a product recommendation, typically by a celebrity, athlete, or other public figure.

**entrepreneur:** a person who organizes and manages any enterprise, especially a business, usually with considerable initiative and at financial risk.

**falsetto:** a man singing in an unnaturally high voice, accomplished by creating a vibration at the very edge of the vocal chords.

**genre:** a subgroup or category within a classification, typically associated with works of art, such as music or literature.

**hone, honing:** sharpening or refining a set of skills necessary to achieve success or perform a specific task.

**icon:** a symbol that represents something, such as a team, a religious person, a location, or an idea.

**innovation:** the introduction of something new or different; a brand-new feature or upgrade to an existing idea, method, or item.

**instrumental:** serving as a crucial means, agent, or tool; of, relating to, or done with an instrument or tool.

**jingle:** a short verse, tune, or slogan used in advertising to make a product easily remembered.

**mogul:** someone considered to be very important, powerful, and in charge; a term usually associated with heads of businesses in the television, movie studio, or recording industries.

**performing arts:** skills that require public performance, as acting, singing, or dancing.

**philanthropy:** goodwill to fellow members of the human race; an active effort to promote human welfare.

**public relations:** the activity or job of providing information about a particular person or organization to the public so that people will regard that person or organization in a favorable way.

**sampler:** a digital or electronic musical instrument, related to a synthesizer, that uses samples, or sound recordings, of real instruments (trumpet, violin, piano, etc.) mixed with excerpts of recorded songs and other interesting sounds (sirens, ocean waves, construction noises, car horns, etc.) that are stored digitally and can be replayed by a triggering device, like a sequencer, electronic drums, or a MIDI keyboard.

**single:** a music recording having two or more tracks that is shorter than an album, EP, or LP; also, a song that is particularly popular, independent of other songs on the same album or by the same artist.

# Further Reading

Beckles, Hilary MCD. *Rihanna: Barbados World-Gurl in Global Popular Culture*. The University of the West Indies Press, 2015.

Govan, Chloe. *Rihanna: Rebel Flower*. Omnibus Press, 2012.

Henwood, Simon and Alexander Vauthier. *Rihanna*. Rizzoli, 2010.

Meseke, Mitch. *The Illustrated Guide to Hip-Hop A–Z*. Independently published, 2017.

Perry, Nicholas. *Rihanna: All the Ins and Outs*. CreateSpace Independent Publishing Platform, 2016.

# Internet Resources

**www.billboard.com**
*The official site of Billboard Music, with articles about artists, chart information, and more.*

**www.thefader.com/**
*Official website for a popular New York City–based music magazine.*

**www.hiphopweekly.com**
*A young adult hip-hop magazine.*

**thesource.com/**
*Website for a bi-monthly magazine that covers hip-hop and pop culture.*

**www.vibe.com/**
*Music and entertainment website and a member of Billboard Music, a division of Billboard-Hollywood Reporter Media Group.*

**www.rihannanow.com/**
*Rihanna's official website is the source for all news, updates, upcoming initiatives, and information about Rihanna.*

74 *Rihanna*
HIP-HOP & R&B

# Citations

"We've been prepping for the tour…" by Rihanna. Vena, Jocelyn. "Rihanna Preps for 'Daring' World Tour." December 03, 2009.

"I love everything about her…" by Kendrick Lamar. Dandridge-Lemco, Ben. "Kendrick Lamar Speaks on Rihanna Collaboration and Why This Album Isn't about Trump." *The FADER*. April 21, 2017.

"…new dimension…" by Carlos Santana. W., Q. K. "DJ Khaled, Rihanna & Bryson Tiller's 'Wild Thoughts' Approved by Carlos Santana." HotNewHipHop. June 21, 2017.

"…drop and give her ten…" by Shontelle. Cwelich, Lorraine. "Shontelle on Being Rihanna's Drill Sergeant." *Elle*. August 29, 2017.

"…Puma Suede creeper…" Mercer, Amirah. "How Rihanna's Puma Creeper Became the Year's Must-Have Shoe." *Vanity Fair*. May 27, 2016.

"…sold out online…" Mercer, "How Rihanna's Puma …*Vanity Fair*.

"I really got to play…" by Rihanna. Niven, Lisa. "Rihanna for MAC." *Vogue*. August 23, 2017.

"Fenty Beauty was created for…" by Rihanna. "Fenty Beauty." Accessed September 24, 2017.

"3.7 times as many strong brand endorsement…" Riley, David. "Rihanna Is the Most Marketable of All Big-Name Celebrities." NPD Group. January 13, 2016.

"Seeing artists such as Rihanna…" by Grazia Chiuri, Artistic Director for Dior. Samaha, Barry. "Christian Dior Partners with Rihanna's Clara Lionel Foundation." *Forbes*, February 28, 2017.

"…want to see what else…" by Rihanna. "Rihanna speaks about *Battleship* role." BBC News. April 09, 2012.

"It was both important to me…" by Rihanna. Murray, Cori. "Rihanna Talks 'Home' and How She Related to Her Animated Character, Tip." Essence.com. April 02, 2015.

"I have felt like an outsider…" Murray, "Rihanna Talks 'Home'…" Essence.com.

"She was so committed…" by Carlton Cuse, Executive Producer. Birnbaum, Debra. "'Bates Motel': Rihanna Makes Her Debut as Marion Crane." *Variety*. March 21, 2017.

"…perfect collision of creativity and fate…" by Carlton Cuse and Kerry Ehrin, Executive Producers. Abrams, Natalie. "'Bates Motel' Books Rihanna in Janet Leigh Role." EW.com. July 22, 2016.

"I loved it. I thought…" by Rihanna. "Rihanna Opens Up about 'Valerian' Role." *Rap-Up*. July 04, 2017.

"…look[ed] like they're in a heist…" by Rihanna fan. Franich, Darren, and Nicole Sperling. "Rihanna and Lupita Nyong'o Will Literally Costar in a Buddy Movie Directed by Ava DuVernay for Netflix." EW.com. May 22, 2017.

"My success started as my dream…" by Rihanna. Bailey, Alyssa. "Here's Every Word of Rihanna's Humanitarian of the Year Speech at Harvard." *Elle*. August 29, 2017.

"We're all human…" by Rihanna. Zamora, Christian. "Rihanna Opened Her Harvard Humanitarian Award Speech with 'So I Made It to Harvard…'" BuzzFeed. Accessed September 24, 2017.

"She's someone I've been in love with…" by Drake. Jang, Meena. "MTV VMAs: Drake Presents Rihanna with the Michael Jackson Video Vanguard Award." *Hollywood Reporter*. August 28, 2016.

"Read Drake, Rihanna's Heartfelt Video Vanguard Award VMAs Speeches." *Rolling Stone*, August 29, 2016.

"The lack of access…" by Rihanna. "Home Page." Clara Lionel Foundation. Accessed September 24, 2017.

"Thank you Mr. President…" by Rihanna. "Rihanna Meets with French President for Education Foundation." *Vibe*, July 26, 2017.

# Educational Video Links

# Photo Credits

# Index

# Index

# Index

## Author's Biography

Panchami Boyd is a graduate of Western University, and she loves to read, write, listen to music, and travel. She loves to learn new things, and is almost always buried under a new book. Learn more at https://www.writeraccess.com/writer/21187/.